By Pete Boyle
of
Have-a-word.com

Disclaimer

Although the author has made every effort to ensure that the information in this book was correct at press time, the author does not assume and hereby disclaim any liability to any party for any loss, damage, or disruption caused by errors or omissions, whether such errors or omissions result from negligence, accident, or any other cause.

Table of Contents

Introduction

It's the same story the world over.

Every friendship group has that one guy who nails every interview. The girl with all the connections who never has to look for work. And finally that one lucky chap you love to hate. The one who falls out of one job and into the next, often with a healthy pay increase to accompany his career change.

It's frustrating, right? All you can do is stand in awe and envy of these people. You're the worker of the group. The one who get's their head down, puts in the hours and has to graft for every single thing you've earned.

That work ethic is an admirable trait, it's got you to where you are today. But you want a little of the luck your friends have, something to make your job search that little bit easier.

Well, there's something you need to know about your 'lucky' friends.

They aren't really that lucky.

The guy who nails the interviews has worked his ass off to perfect his interpersonal skills. The lady with the connections, she's out there week in week out meeting industry pros and growing her network. And the last guy, well, more often than not he's just a great bullshitter.

Each of those people has spent countless hours building and perfecting their skills. They've put in the laborious work and are now reaping the benefits.

I'm here to offer you a shortcut. I'm going to share the secrets I've learned through countless hours of practice as a freelance copywriter. The skills that will help you increase the effectiveness of your resumés.

"But hold on, what's a freelancer doing giving resumé advice?" you ask. I work for myself, right? I don't need to send resumés to clients and worry about getting interviews.

Well, that's a half truth. Sure, I don't need to send resumés in the traditional sense, but I have to pitch myself to clients every single day. I send around five to ten emails and portfolio samples to potential clients every week. Each one's sole intention to sell myself and my skills.

Why do I send these resumé like emails? So they'll hire me to write more materials that sell their company or goods.

The entirety of my job is using words to sell products, build reputations and convince readers to take a chance on what's been laid out in front of them.

I've written sales letters for top end products, created marketing materials for multinationals and written more than a few professional resumés, corporate and LinkedIn bios in my time.

Professionals understand that copywriters know how to sell with words. And that's what I want to impart unto you. The secrets of the trade. The how and the why businesses and professionals hire me to write their marketing and sales material for them. Because let's face it, that's all a resume is.

It's a sales letter with you as the product.

I can't teach you the ins and outs of copywriting in one short eBook, but I can give a crash course in resumé persuasion.

If you follow the principles outlined in this eBook you'll not only have more employers responding to your applications, but you'll be the envy of Mr Interview, Ms Network and Captain Bullshit.

You'll be the Resumé King. The one your friends come to when they need help polishing their resumé. Trust me, it's not an empty boast, it's the science of advertising.

Enough with the prattle, let's get straight into it.

Common Mistakes that Ruin Your Resumé

This eBook is going to serve as a practical guide to creating a compelling resumé. One which persuades your recruiter to take the action you want and inviting you to interview.

As a practical guide you'll be walked step by step through a proven process that highlights how to understand and exceed the expectations of your targeted employer.

However, the downfall with practical guides is they sometimes gloss over useful advice and information. The step by step approach is great for detail, but omits more general advice.

To cover all bases and ensure subsequent steps are taken without making the same mistakes as your competition, I'll be leading with a few general guidelines that should always be followed.

Relying on Resumé Templates

Don't rely on resumé templates you can download from the internet. They're generally not bad but aren't going to help you stand out from the crowd and make an impression. After all, there's probably dozens, if not hundreds, of other job seekers out there who are using the exact same template.

Use them for inspiration, but always create your own.

Personal Information

Despite what you've been told, not all personal information is relevant. You're not writing your biography for a dating site, you're applying for a job.

Ask yourself what's truly relevant to the job. Does your penchant for Sunday kite surfing make you more suitable for the role? Are you a great hire because you play squash every week?

No.

Unless you're applying to a kite surfing or squash related business they have no relevance and take up valuable room that could be used to highlight professional strengths employers want.

The same goes for your social media accounts. Your employer doesn't want or need to see your Facebook, Twitter or Pinterest posts. List your LinkedIn but nothing else.

Photo

There's a growing trend to include a headshot with your resumé which, if we're being honest, is tacky and doesn't add any value or quality. If you're not applying to be a model or actor/actress then a headshot isn't needed.

Education Information

So you had some great scores for high school exams. Well done you! But how is that relevant to the position you're applying for?

Generally speaking the only educational information you need to include is your most recent achievement.

The exception to the rule are positions in academia where the details of your educational path to your current qualification might be important.

Work History

Don't include every position you've ever held. Jobs from way back often have no bearing on your current application.

Unless there's a relevant achievement from the time you spent working in retail while at school, omit these useless jobs.

You'll also want to cut the months you worked at each job. You've limited time and space to make an impression with a resume. All those mentions of June 2014 - March 2016 take up valuable space that could be better utilized. Use the year, nothing else.

Listing your reason for departing a company is best avoided. You may think it helps explain and perhaps legitimize your need to break from a former employer, but it just wastes space. If employers are interested why, they'll ask at the interview.

References

Recruiters expect you to have references. You don't need to tell them you have some or that they're available upon request. It's another waste of space which could be better put to use.

Sending Your Resumé to the Wrong Person

Sending a resumé does not constitute being productive.

You might feel great after a day where you sent 20 resumés to potential employers, but if you're sending them to the wrong people within the business or to industries you've not tailored your resumé for, you're going to get zero responses.

Make sure you're sending your resumé to the right person (a topic covered in detail in the free email course).

Objective

An objective in your resume is useless.

Recruiters know you're applying for a position because you've sent them your resume. If you've something important to say about the position or your experience, do it in your cover letter.

The Five Kinds of Resumé

The average recruiter spends only six seconds reviewing a resumé before making a decision on whether the candidate deserves more of their time[1].

Crazy right. Your resume is judged within six seconds of the recruiter picking it up.

But recruiters are busy people often having to sift through hundreds of resumés for a single position. They don't have time to check every application in detail. If your resumé is too difficult to read or doesn't fit their expectations, it's going in the trash..

One of the keys to capturing and holding recruiter attention is in how you format your resumé. You've got to understand the different formats and designs and their pros and cons if you want to stand out from the multitudes of applicants.

Below I've outlined the five types of resumé format you can adopt and their various pros and cons. Consider these carefully as the different formats are immediately recognizable and could have a huge impact (positive or negative) on the effectiveness of your application.

The Chronological Resumé

This is arguably the most popular format for resumés and is nothing more than a simple list of the positions you've held. You'll start with your current job and work your way back through your work history to the last relevant job.

Advantages

Chronological resumés are easy to write. All you've got to do is list where you've worked and what you've achieved whilst in your different positions. They're perfect for you if you've had a long and steady work history.

Disadvantages

If you've any career gaps they stick out like a sore thumb on a chronological resumé. They're also a poor choice for fresh graduates who have little to no work experience or those seeking a career change where previous experience has little relevancy to their new industry.

Many make the mistake of failing to highlight key achievements with chronological resumés. Knowing you were a 'product manager' at X Corporation is great, but it doesn't help identify the key skills that make you perfect for the position you're applying to.

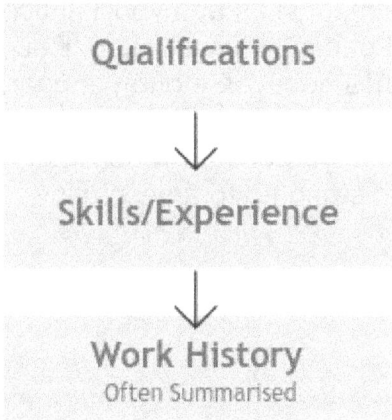

The Functional Resumé

Functional resumés are skills based. They focus on your ability rather than your employment history. Generally speaking they gloss over the dates of your employment which isn't a bad approach per sé, but does require a lot of context and content to back up your claims.

Advantages

Functional resumés are a good option for those in a handful of positions.

1. Those fresh out of college
2. Those with gaps in their employment history
3. Those looking to change their career and/or industry

Focusing on your strengths and abilities makes for a better connection to the role you're applying for in the above situations where a chronological order might highlight your spotty employment past or experience in an unrelated field.

Disadvantages

Check any online resumé form or the guidelines on recruitment sites and you'll notice that functional resumés aren't particularly well liked. Recruiters dislike functional resumés because it often appears as though the applicant has something to hide. They're usually filled with buzzwords and fluff, the type of stuff which looks great at a cursory glance but fails to stand up to any scrutiny.

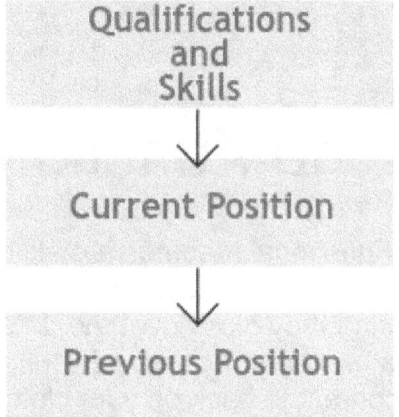

The Combination Resumé

No prizes for guessing what this is!

Combination resumés attempt to combine the best parts of both a chronological and functional resumé. Generally speaking it follows closer to a chronological format. It leads with your key skills and strengths, but follows by a reverse chronology of your employment history.

Advantages

It has the best of both worlds. It shows your full chronological history to appease the expectations of the hiring party but also allows you to highlight the key skills and attributes you can bring to the table.

Disadvantages

These are longer than the average resumé. Sometimes your work history begins on the second page which might not sound bad, but could be the difference between a recruiter reading your resumé and throwing it in the trash.

Most recruiters lose interest after the first page and won't look at anything past the second (remember, you only have six seconds to make an impression). The major downfall of this approach is that you're taking a chance on your recruiter's attention span.

The Visual Resumé

Visual resumés are the new kid on the block. They break from tradition and are a great way to visually represent your skills and work history. They take their lead from infographics and are an ideal choice for those in design fields or who are looking for employment from young tech startups.

Advantages

Ad agencies across the world realized long ago that one of the best methods for capturing and retaining user attention is to make content more visually appealing. The visual resume does exactly that.

A well designed visual resumé is a perfect way to highlight your skills and let your recruiter know in seconds what it is you can bring to the table.

Disadvantages

Visual resumés are often brightly colored and loud. They're great, but only for a small percentage of career paths. A financial institution or other traditional organization wouldn't appreciate a brightly colored, over the top and fun resumé. They have their traditions and are often unwilling to break from them.

They're also hard to design for those not skilled in Illustrator.

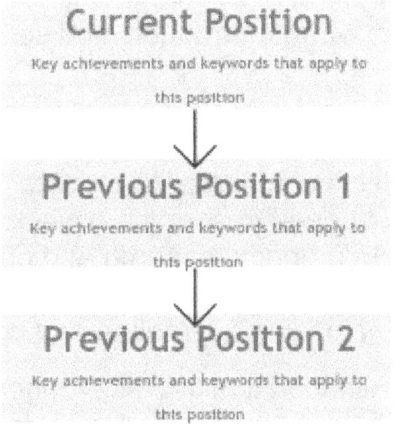

The Copywriting Resumé

This is my method, the one you'll learn about in this eBook.

The copywriting resumé follows the format of the chronological resumé. We're utilizing that format because it's the most popular and well received by recruiters the world over.

However, we're also deviating from the accepted chronological path by adding some much needed razzle-dazzle.

Advantages

It follows the most accepted format and so, when well optimized, is likely to capture attention in those first vital six seconds. It speaks to the needs of the business and is sure to get you noticed.

It follows the guidelines set out by the world's most famous copywriters. The marketers who not only know how to write compelling content, but have done so to sell billions of dollars worth of products and services.

Disadvantages

It's much harder to produce a copywriting resumé. You're going to need to spend a considerable amount of time and effort to properly research and optimize your resume. You can't take the generic approach so many do with their resumé of downloading a template and changing a few details.

Although it might take longer, it's definitely worth the hassle if you want to find your dream job.

Step 1 - Why Your Current Mindset is Wrong (and How to Change It)

The first step in the copywriting approach is undoubtedly the most important.

You need to discard your current way of thinking, the advice you've received and the 'wisdom' you've read on writing a resume and applying for jobs. All those articles, pieces of personal advice and guidance you've received from friends, family and 'career advice experts' needs to be forgotten.

Why?

Because more often than not, it's terrible advice.

How many times have you been told to highlight what you've done in your employment history? A lot, right?

Now ask yourself how much of what you've done is truly interesting, groundbreaking or helps you stand out from the other applicants? I'm willing to bet it's a comparatively small percentage of information.

Now, here's the hard truth.

Deep down, employers don't care about what you've done in your past. They don't care about you. They don't care about your former employers.

All they care about is what you can do for them.

If I've learned one thing as a copywriter it's how selfish we all are.

No one buys a new camera because of the hard work the product development team has put into developing a new technology. They buy it because they want clearer pictures for themselves.

No one buys a new car because some poor soul sat for months designing a sexy new chassis. They purchase it because it's going to make them feel sexier, get them to where they're going faster or because it's a safer vehicle for their family.

In both our personal or professional lives we're all always looking for how a purchase (or in this case a hire) can benefit us.

It makes me sound like a cynical bastard and the world seem a little less happy, but it's true. And the sooner you realize this the better off you'll be.

Stop thinking of your employment history as 'what you've done' and start thinking about how what you've done can help the business you're applying for? Focus on your achievements.

You didn't talk to new clients.

You helped the company secure $X in new business/grow revenue by X%.

You didn't help with the filing.

You implemented a new filing approach saving the company $X per year in wasted man-hour payments.

You didn't organize deliveries.

You successfully supervised $40,000 of stock every month and ensured safe arrival and thus payment.

Too many resumés focus on the boring, mundane and menial.

If you instead focus on what was achieved through your actions it makes it far more appealing to the hiring party. They don't see vague claims that have nothing to do with their business, they see the results you brought your former employer.

Nothing is sexier and more appealing to a businessman than thinking they're getting a great deal and increasing the value of their business. Focus on your achievements and you position yourself as a provider of value.

The focus of your resumé no longer lists what you've done, but rather highlights what you can do. The implication of course is that you can replicate these results for your new employer.

Questions to Ask Yourself

Of course turning your normal day to day actions into achievement focused resumé copy isn't easy. You can't just spin X,Y and Z into an amazing sales pitch of your abilities. To help get you on the right path I've included a few questions you need to ask yourself in relation to your previous work history.

- Did you increase sales, revenue or other key metrics?
  - If yes, by how much?
- How many people did you work with, employ or manage?
- Did you implement a new strategy or idea?
  - If so, what was the result?
- Did you decrease any negative metrics like debt, wasted time, turnaround times etc?
  - How and by how much?

The basic formulae you now need to employ when thinking of your achievements follows the below pattern.

I did **[action]** which [increased/decreased/improved/etc] by **[quantifiable amount]**.

Step 2 - Perfecting Your Resumé Design

How you display your information is key to breaking through the six second attention span of the average recruiter. You want to quickly grab attention and the best way to do that is to place the most compelling piece of information in the area that initially draws the eye.

This is something I have to do in my professional life quite often, especially when devising a new product landing page. A landing page is one of those web pages which advertises a product or service and tries to elicit the submission of an email address or bank details for payment.

Copywriters know we only have eight seconds to capture attention and keep the prospect on our page[2]. To help us combat this and ensure we place compelling content in the correct sections our first step is to devise a wireframe.

What is a Wireframe?

A wireframe is used to work out the visual hierarchy of your page. It highlights design flaws. Should you put those two key pieces of information close to one another or are they easier to understand with a little space between them?

Think of it as a guide for attention mapping and understanding where the shortcomings in your designs are. There's plenty of services online that can help you devise a wireframe but you'd be just as well served with a pen and paper.

All you're really looking for at this stage is a basic outline of what information is going to go where so you can understand the general flow of your resumé and whether there's any major gaps or issues that need addressing.

The below is an example of three different wireframes that follow popular formats. Play around with your design to devise a design that helps highlight your key skills in the most

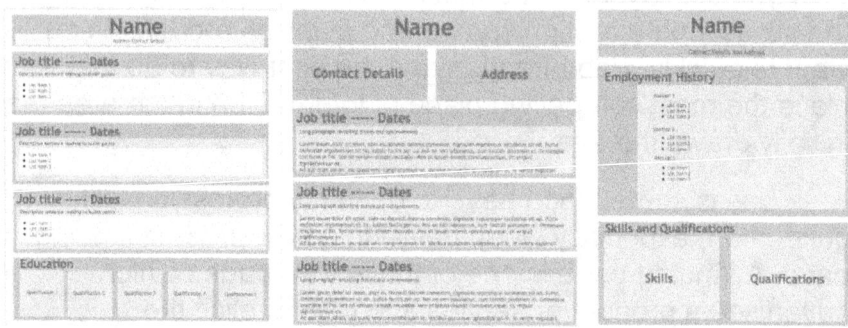

unique and easy to assimilate fashion.

Remember, you don't need any fancy software for this, a pen and paper is just as good.

But Wait! Before You Start Drawing, Know This

Before you start devising your wireframe I want to point out exactly what you need to consider when designing your resumé for maximum impact.

Take a look at the below image.

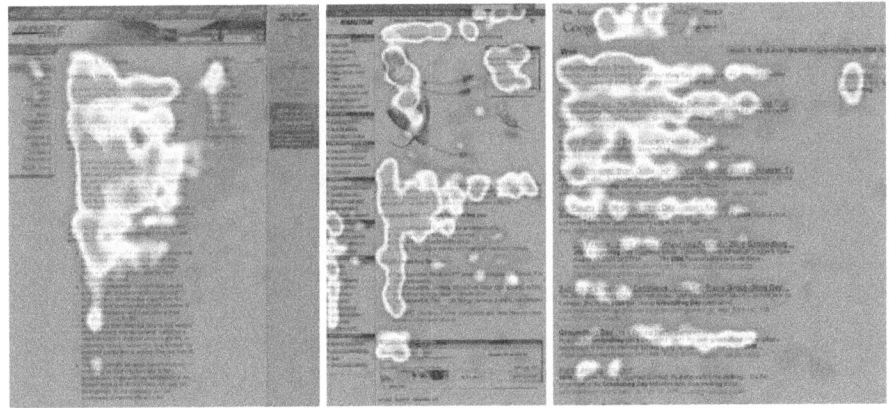

The above is what's called a heat map. This particular heat map is from the Nielsen Norman Group and highlights the average person's reading patterns[3].

You can see that when it comes to large volumes of text, there's a distinct F shape to the way users read. Knowing how users read will help you choose the best areas to place your key information.

Whilst the above is a good general guideline, it's not specifically aimed at resumés. Fortunately there's a resume specific eye tracking heat map from the Business Insider[4] which I've included below.

You can see that there's still a vague F shape to the attention.

What's also interesting is how the resumé on the right held the recruiter's attention for a longer period. I'd wager this is down to the better formatting.

They've taken the time to ensure an easily scannable, succinct format making it easier for the recruiter to quickly scan the information for key points.

What to Consider When Creating Your Wireframe

The primary consideration with your wireframe at this stage should be the general organization of information. Look at the above heat maps and use them to structure your resume plan in a way that's easy for the recruiter to pick out key information.

However, you'll also want to consider the below. It's still early days on the design side but the earlier you get a basic plan worked out the easier things will be.

1 - Remember the F shape for attention

Use it to choose where your key information is going to be placed. Remember those six seconds of attention, choose wisely to persuade the recruiter you're worth more of their time.

2 - Make it scannable

Long blocks of text are difficult to scan for key information. Six seconds isn't a long time and you can be damn sure the recruiter isn't going to be reading every word.

The effective use of whitespace demonstrated in the right hand resumé above has made it easier for the recruiter to find key information and has ultimately held their attention for longer

3 - Include all elements

Be sure that your wireframe includes everything. You don't want to have a killer design only to have it ruined later because you forgot to take your contact details or email address placement into consideration.

4 - Remain flexible

As mentioned it's early days yet. You might find later on that a piece of information becomes less, or more, important. Remain flexible with your design so you can amend it to adapt to any future changes.

Step 3 - How to Properly Research the Industry

Entrepreneurial reality shows are littered with people who haven't taken heed of the following advice.

Dragon's Den, The Apprentice and Shark Tank all have competitors who think they've got something special, something the world needs and can no longer do without.

More often than not, these guys are wrong. Their amazing idea has no market.

They've failed to do their research and don't know what the end user is crying out for or what problems they need solved.

All they do is think of an idea and rush it through to development which is a surefire way to fail.

Resumés often suffer from a similar problem. Too many job seekers think they know what their targeted employer wants so they rush through their resumé and cover letter only to find that really, they had no idea what would make them a good choice for the role.

Your end user is your target employer. You need to know exactly what it is they're looking for. The only way to do that is to fully research the industry and the job role you're applying for.

Thankfully it's not as difficult as you might think. To get the best idea of what's required there's three websites you need to become comfortable with.

LinkedIn

GlassDoor

Your target company's website

You're going to use these three in conjunction with the job advertisement to create a resumé that hits all the right points and focuses on the skills your targeted employer needs.

What to Look for on LinkedIn

LinkedIn is a treasure trove for job hunters. Most only use it to find jobs and add random people to their network, but if you know what to look for you can find so much information which can take your resumé to the next level.

Your first port of call on LinkedIn should be other people who work in the company you're applying to. Stop by their profiles in the below order.

Group 1 - People who already do the job you're applying for

Group 2 - Their immediate superior

Group 3 - The recruiter/HR person

Group 4 - The CEO/Founder

Spend a little time going through each person's page. You're looking to pull out the below key information from each group.

Group 1

You're looking here for keywords pertaining to the role.

How do these people describe the job and their own skill set? Look at the language and the tone they use when describing themselves and their current position.

These people have successfully achieved what you're trying to, so follow their lead.

Group 2

This is the person who will most likely have final sign off on whether you're hired. Look for how they describe themselves. Do they use any power words about their ability or the job? It's a good indication of the kind of values they're also looking for in their employees.

Group 3

What you really want from this person is their name and email address. Instead of following the same procedure as everyone else you can send them direct email which opens with their name instead of "Dear Sir/Madam". That little bit of personalization is a small step but is proven to increase email

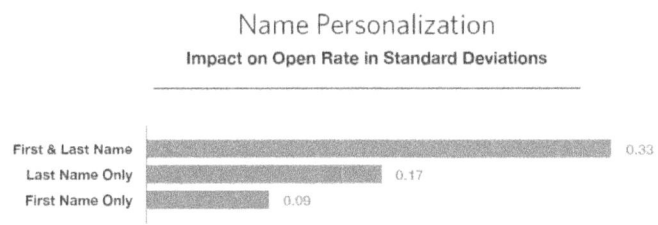

open rates and engagement[5].

Group 4

What does the head honcho have to say about the business? If it's also the person who's founded the company you can get a good indication of what company environment they're trying to foster. Are they light hearted, fun and focus on growth? Are they serious and financially motivated?

Look into their habits and language to get an idea of the kind of people they want in their company. What the big boss wants will filter down through every level.

When you're looking through these different profiles you need to mark down some key information in a spreadsheet. You can create your own or download the one I've created for you (there's a text link in the references section of the book).

If you're creating your own you need to include the following columns and populate them with the suggestions below.

Language Used

The language used is incredibly important. You want to know what adjectives and phrases are repeatedly mentioned across profiles. These are the 'power words' we'll be implementing when writing your resumé. The more frequently a word/adjective/phrase appears, the more important it is.

Achievements Made/Problems Overcome

What achievements do the employees consider important? What problems do they think were important enough to mention? This gives you an insight into the values they're looking for. If they list a lot of financial achievements, you'll want to focus your own resumé on your own financial achievements.

What They Want

LinkedIn is a little difficult to discern what people want. Everyone's trying to blow their own horn and it makes it difficult to discern anything other than their achievements. You still need to include it in your spreadsheet though as it's important for the next step.

What to Look for on Glass Door

If you're not aware of Glass Door it's a site where employees can offer anonymous reviews of the business they work for. You'll find some glowing reviews and some scathing remarks; both of which are incredibly useful for you.

You need to search for the company you're targeting and read through as many reviews as you can. Use the positive information you find to bolster and pad out the information already in your spreadsheet.

There's often lots of references to the working atmosphere and the nature of the business. Great information for tailoring your resumé.

Glass Door is where you'll find enough information to populate the final column in your spreadsheet. You'll often see reviews where people complain about a lack of organization in sector X, Y or Z or how there's an ongoing problem with finance/reception etc.

You can bet your ass that if someone has taken to the internet to complain about something it's a well known problem within the company. If you have skills that can solve that problem, be sure to include it in your resume. You might just be exactly what the employer is looking for.

What to Look for on the Company Page

Businesses live or die on their reputations. A good marketing angle, a grandiose claim and a little bit of proof can be the difference between huge success or resounding failure for many businesses.

Successful businesses understand this and so fill their websites with their biggest successes and greatest achievements for potential clients to see. It's a viable method of attracting new business, but it also permits a snapshot of company life and the values they deem important.

If you can align your values and skills with those your target employer believes paramount to success, you're halfway to success.

More often than not you'll find a good deal of information on achievements and successes or hints to key company ideals on the company's about/history page.

Here's the homepage of Alphabet, the parent company for Google in which I've highlighted some interesting phrases.

is for Google

As Sergey and I wrote in the original founders letter 11 years ago, "Google is not a conventional company. We do not intend to become one." As part of that, we also said that you could expect us to make "smaller bets in areas that might seem very speculative or even strange when compared to our current businesses." From the start, we've always strived to do more, and to do important and meaningful things with the resources we have.

We did a lot of things that seemed crazy at the time. Many of those crazy things now have over a billion users, like Google Maps, YouTube, Chrome, and Android. And we haven't stopped there. We are still trying to do things other people think are crazy but we are super excited about.

We've long believed that over time companies tend to get comfortable doing the same thing, just making incremental changes. But in the technology industry, where revolutionary ideas drive the next big growth areas, you need to be a bit uncomfortable to stay relevant.

The highlighted phrases give me the impression that Google looks for employees who are entrepreneurial, unconventional yet passionate in their approach and are willing to step outside of their comfort zone.

All little things, but add up to some key insights into the business and how you can adapt your resumé to their needs.

Put time aside to look through a business's web page. Any pages or articles that outline the ethos of the business, past achievements they're proud of or their portfolio page and how they describe past projects and clients.

It's not as cut and dry as LinkedIn or GlassDoor. You're going to need to think outside the box a little and discern how a claim made on a website could apply to you and what particular attribute that success relied on.

Whilst not as easy as some of the other research methods, it's pretty damn important.

Don't Half Ass Your Research

Your research is the most important stage of creating an incredible resumé. Without taking this stage seriously you're doing little more than taking a stab in the dark.

Your research is going to be the difference between a crappy, generic resumé and one which hits all the right points and establishes you as the best person for the job.

Whatever you do, don't half ass your research.

Step 4 - Turning Your Research into a Compelling Resumé

The good news is the laborious monotony that is research is over.

You should now know:

1 - The words those in your target business/position use to describe the role

2 - The kind of atmosphere that's being fostered at your target company

3 - The achievements they deem important and brag worthy

4 - The key values they look for in employees

Your job now is to turn your research into some absolutely killer content for your own resumé.

The mistake most make at this point is to immediately write their resumé. They jump back and forth between research and writing creating a disjointed flow. You might have all the right words and achievements, but if it's a difficult read the recruiter won't give it their full attention.

Read through all of your research a few times throughout the day. Think about the best ways you can adapt your experience and achievements to the needs and expectations of the target business. That's all you need to do for today. Review and analyze.

Once you've internalized what they're looking for and have a good idea how you can tailor your experience to their needs it's time to sit down and write. I recommend a 24 hour gap between the start of your analysis and writing.

Before you do start writing, read through and understand the below:

1 - Write Conversationally

Good copywriters always write their copy as if it's aimed at an individual person. Writing a letter that sounds like it's addressed to a dozen or more people fails to make an impact.

You've got to imagine that you're having a conversation with the recruiter at a job fair or networking event. It gets rid of the overly formal style many use in there resumés and makes it an easier and more engaging read.

Imagine you're sat across the table from a recruiter and are explaining what it is you've achieved. Put those words onto paper and you've done the hardest part.

2 - Don't Brag, Don't be Modest

Brag and you're an arrogant dick. Be too modest and you lack conviction.

Don't try to wax lyrical about what you've achieved but don't play it down either. State what you've achieved in plain, simple terms and move on. It's the only way to highlight what you've achieved without coming across as arrogant.

3 - Ditch the Pronouns

"I've done this. I've done that." wastes valuable space.

The only subject of your resumé is you. Recruiters know everything listed is in reference to your past. Constantly referring to yourself in the first or third person is a waste of space.

4 - Avoid Generic Buzzwords

You're a *go-getter*. You're *motivated*. You're a *team player*. All terms proven to turn recruiters off your otherwise awesome resumé[6].

These are not quantifiable terms. Change the focus and use your achievements to display these qualities.

Saying you spearheaded a new project that exceeded $10,000 in revenue shows you're a motivated go-getter. It leaves no question as to your ability whereas outright stating your qualities begs the question 'how'.

As a general rule of thumb, if it's a word a competitor on The Apprentice would use, it's not for you.

5 - The Three S's of Compelling Content

Recruiters are busy, we know this from their goldfish-esque attention spans. They don't want to read through huge blocks of text to find one key point. When creating your resumé follow the three S rule. Everything you write should be:

Simple

Short

Specific

Try to explain your achievements in as few words as possible. Get right to the point and waste no time.

Your First Draft Will be Terrible… But That's OK

What you write will likely be terrible. First drafts always are. What's most important is to follow the basic wireframe you created and the various writing rules I've outlined.

If you properly internalized your research and considered how to adapt your achievements to the position then this stage shouldn't be too difficult.

Just remember to write as you'd speak to the recruiter. Don't worry too much about the rules outlined, if you make a mistake and include a generic buzzword or something isn't specific enough right now, leave it.

You'll clear it up and make it shine in the editing stage.

The key part for this step is to get the bulk of your resumé down onto paper.

Step 5- 6 Simple Editing Tricks to Take Your Resumé to the Next Level

It's during the editing phase that everything comes together.

You'll have the opportunity to remove any irrelevant achievements, duties or generic buzzwords that slipped through your filter during the writing phase. This is where you tighten your writing and the focus to deliver the same impactful message in as few words as possible.

Before you start editing you've got to keep the below questions in mind to ask when you read through what you've created:

1 - Does this resumé represent me as the perfect candidate for this position.

2 - Is this an experience/duty or an achievement?

3 - Is this necessary and relevant

You've got to kill your darlings when you edit. You might like the way something sounds or think it makes you look a certain way, but if it fails in any of the above questions then it's got to either be amended or cut.

Exercise Extreme Brevity

Most resumés I read could easily cut 40% - 50% of the words without losing any meaning or impact. There's a peculiar and misguided belief of thinking the more depth you provide to an explanation the better it will be received and understood.

But remember the six second attention rule. You've got next to no time to make an impression. Cut any words that aren't absolutely 100% necessary or don't support your message.

<u>Here's an article that goes into great detail on brevity</u> and how you can cut the meaningless word from your work[7]. Below you'll find a quick summary of the key points to creating effective content.

1 - Make Everything as Long as it Needs to be, but No Longer

Get your message across as succinctly as possible.

Instead of saying:

"While working for company X I managed to implement a new program that increased customer acquisition by 50%"

Say:

"Implemented new strategy that increased customer acquisition by 50%"

The second sentence is 50% shorter and has the exact same meaning. It's listed under your chronological employment history so recruiters know which company you were at and there's no need for pronouns because this is your resume.

You've got your point across in half the time without losing any relevance or impact.

2 - Cut Weak Adjective and Verbs

The word 'very' should be cut from your vocabulary. You want to appear confident and very is an extremely weak word. Read your sentences and ask if you can either cut the word completely from your vocabulary or replace it for something with more oomph.

You're not very interested in something. You're interested.

You're not very good. You're exceptional.

You're not very capable. You're accomplished.

The same approach should be applied to your sentence structure.

Using active voice and action verbs gives your writing more impact. Take a look at the below and tell me what's more captivating.

I had to analyze monthly reports

I analyzed monthly reports

I was tasked with collecting client details

I collected client details

Had to effectively delegate work to other members of the team

Delegated work to team members

In each instance the second option not only has more impact, but delivers the same message in fewer words.

Always use active voice and action verbs. If you're still not sure what an action verb is, here's a handy example that also demonstrates the concept.

- An action verb **is a verb that represents** an action
- An action verb **represents** an action

3 - Use Bullet Points

Bullet points have been marketers go to method for delivering key information in short periods of time for years.

Instead of giving your recruiter a block of text to sift through for one or two achievements, pull out the key information and display it as bullet points. Bullet points draw the eye and allow readers to quickly and easily understand what it is you're trying to say. You can either go overboard with your writing and create a rather intimidating and unappealing wall of text for recruiters to read, or you can spend a couple of minutes reading your work and reformatting it not just for easier reading, but for greater impact. Trust me when I say your recruiter will be far more appreciative of this formatting approach and will give your resume more of their time.

That's a big paragraph right? Be honest, did you read it all? No? Good. That proves my point. Tell me what's easier to read, the above paragraph or the below bullet points that outline the exact same information.

- Don't write paragraphs
- Pull out key information to display as bullet points
- Makes your resumé easier to read and easier for recruiter to spot key achievements

- Quickly spotting achievements will ensure you get more than the cursory six second glance

4 - Make Use of Power Words

Copywriters use power words to elicit emotion. We want people to feel a certain way because, if we can elicit certain emotions readers are more likely to take the action we want them to. You'll see sales materials that use words including free, incredible, agony, danger etc.

All of these words are chosen and carefully placed to make the reader feel something. But they do more than elicit an emotion, they're there to create a connection. When people read language that explains their own feelings or represents their needs it builds trust[8].

You're not playing with emotions on a resumé but you can create a connection, one which helps place you as the primary contender for the role.

You've got a spreadsheet that's full of information explaining the exact words current employees and the business itself uses to describe the role, workplace, working atmosphere and ethos.

Use it to your advantage.

However, be mindful of how you use these words. Don't just list them and expect great results.

If you've settled on a role that requires excellent negotiation skills don't say, "*expert negotiator*" or "*skilled in negotiation*". That's too obvious and offers no proof.

You need to explain how you've successfully negotiated deals in the past. Focus on your achievements but use the power words you've identified to explain them.

"renegotiated contract saving [company name] $X every year"

Whether your resumé goes direct to the company or via a third party recruiter they'll be on the look out for the key phrases and terms that align with the business's current needs. Use them wisely and you could pull attention directly to your key achievements.

5 - Quantify your Achievements

Vague achievements impress no one.

Saying you "improved a process" or "increased revenue" are too vague. The immediate response to vague claims is to dismiss them as hyperbole.

The recruiter doesn't know to what extent you've improved or increased anything. It could have been by 0.01% or 50%. Because you haven't listed the number the automatic assumption is there's something to hide and the achievement isn't as grand as you claim.

You need to get specific with your achievements. When you're editing your work examine each achievement and decide if a value can be attributed to it. If a value can be attributed, make sure it's the most flattering one.

For instance, saying you increased Coca Cola's revenue by 0.5% sounds like an extremely minor achievement.

But Coca Cola's company is huge. 0.5% equates to over $100 million dollars. Saying you increased revenue by over $100 million is far more impressive than 0.5%.

Always attribute a value to achievements when possible, just ensure you're attributing the most flattering measurement.

Step 6 - The Final Three Point Checklist

The hard work is done.

Your resumé is pretty much ready to go. But I'm not one to take chances, and when it comes to your career, nor should you.

Before you start sending this out to potential employers there's a three point checklist you need to follow.

1 - Don't Rely on Spell Check

Spell check is great at picking up misspelt words. What it often fails to identify are incorrect words. For instance, it's very easy to write mo instead of no. Spellcheck won't list mo as a mistake so you'll end up sending it out to employers.

Spell check also automatically corrects what it assumes to be incorrectly spelt words. Business names are a prime example of words that are often spelt in slightly peculiar ways. It would be incredibly embarrassing for you if spell check automatically changed the name of a former employer or, even worse, the name of the business you're applying to.

Before you do anything you need to read every single word in your resumé out loud. Reading out loud helps to identify problems with the flow of your resumé as well as forcing you to read every single word.

It's much easier to spot any errors and correct them before moving on to the next step.

2 - Give it to a Friend/Family Member

Proofreading your own work is never ideal.

Your brain knows what you wanted to say and will overlook minor typos and errors because it knows what you wanted to say. You need a fresh set of eyes to read your resumé and to specifically look for:

- Spelling and grammar errors
- Errors in syntax
- Any areas that are unclear

Tell whoever reads it to be ruthless in their feedback. It will hurt to have someone tell you your masterpiece is garbage, but better a friend than a potential employer shred your resumé.

3 - Double Check Your Design

One of the first steps in this guide was to create a wireframe. A general design outline dictating where you'd place key information for maximum exposure.

Now that you've finished creating your resumé it's time to check if your key information and largest achievements fall into the areas where attention is most focused.

Refer once again to the heat maps included in Chapter 5. Do your key achievements and most persuasive information fall into the areas where attention is most focused?

If not, see what you can do to move things around and ensure your best bits get the most attention.

STOP! Don't Forget Your FREE Cover Letter Email Course!

This guide should serve as a comprehensive walkthrough on how to produce a compelling resumé that gets you the interview. However, your resumé is only half of the equation.

The other half that needs as detailed an approach as this is the creation of your cover letter.

Your cover letter is going to be the first thing a recruiter sees and is the ideal place to personalize your message to really stand out from the crowd.

To complement the steps outlined in this eBook for resumé creation I've put together a short email course on cover letter writing.

To sign up to the email course simply navigate to **coverlettercourse.com** and follow the on screen instructions.

You'll find a page which will ask for your name and email address. All you've got to do is fill in your details and click the button. Once that's done I'll have the first of the five emails in your inbox within 30 minutes.

Each of the five emails examines a key area of cover letter creation and comes complete with actionable steps to help improve your chances of getting your dream job.

Email Course Outline

Email 1 - How to Make your Cover Letter Work Smarter, Not Harder

Email 2 - The Four Paragraph Template for Cover Letters that Get Noticed

Email 3 - How Speculative Cover Letters Cut the Competition and Put You One Step Ahead

Email 4 - Who Should You Send your Resumé and Cover Letter To (And How to Find their Best Email Address)

Email 5 - The Best Advice to Finding Your Dream Job

If you've enjoyed this book and have found it useful, be sure to sign up to the free email course and you'll get lesson number one within the next 30 minutes.

References

1 - Keeping an Eye on recruiter Behaviour report by The Ladders
http://cdn.theladders.net/static/images/basicSite/pdfs/TheLadders-EyeTracking-StudyC2.pdf

2 - Attention Span Statistics by Statistic Brain
http://www.statisticbrain.com/attention-span-statistics/

3 - F Shaped Pattern for reading Online Content by Jakob Nielsen of The Nielsen Norman Group
https://www.nngroup.com/articles/f-shaped-pattern-reading-web-content/

4 - What Recruiters Look At During The 6 Seconds They Spend On Your Resume by Vivian Giang
http://www.businessinsider.com/heres-what-recruiters-look-at-during-the-6-seconds-they-spend-on-your-resume-2012-4?IR=T

5 - Subject Line Data: Choose Your Words Wisely by Mailchimp
http://blog.mailchimp.com/subject-line-data-choose-your-words-wisely/

6 - Hiring Managers Rank Best and Worst Words to Use in a Résumé by CareerBuilder Survey
http://www.careerbuilder.com/share/aboutus/pressreleasesdetail.aspx?id=pr809&sd=3/13/2014&ed=03/13/2014

7 - The Power of Precision Writing - Why Brevity is Important by Pete Boyle
http://have-a-word.com/why-brevity-is-important/

8 - Linguistic mimicry and trust in text-based CMC by Northwestern University
https://www.researchgate.net/profile/Darren_Gergle/publication/220878924_Linguistic_mimicry_and_trust_in_text-based_CMC/links/0fcfd510be7ce16534000000.pdf

Free Spreadsheet Text Link

https://goo.gl/dqzFBB

Produced By...

This eBook was produced entirely by Pete Boyle of Have-a-word.com.

I'm a freelance copywriter who helps others build their own businesses with words to achieve the professional freedom I've discovered.

If, despite the lessons in this guide, you decide you want to go it alone in the working world but aren't sure where to start, sign up to the mailing list at have-a-word.com.

You'll receive free advice and guidance on how to build your own business in your own time and live your life on your own terms.

www.ingramcontent.com/pod-product-compliance
Lightning Source LLC
Chambersburg PA
CBHW070337190526
45169CB00005B/1940